★ ★ ★ ★ ★ ★ ★ ★ ★ ★

The CLINTONS

★ **Meet the First Family** ★

by Chip Eliot

W9-BMB-166

Watermill Press

★ ★ ★ ★ ★ ★ ★ ★ ★ ★

AMERICA GETS
A NEW FIRST FAMILY

When American voters elected President Bill Clinton, they brought many changes to the nation's capital. One of the biggest changes came in January 1993, when President Clinton and his wife Hillary Rodham Clinton moved into the White House.

President and Mrs. Clinton aren't the only members of the new First Family. For the first time in a dozen years, there's a kid in the White House, 13-year-old Chelsea Clinton. There's even a new presidential pet — a black and white cat named Socks!

For Bill Clinton and his family, the road to the White House was a long one. For Bill Clinton himself, it's the realization of a dream that was born 30 years ago when the President was an Arkansas teenager.

THE MAN FROM HOPE

President Clinton was born William Jefferson Blythe IV on August 19, 1946, in a small Arkansas town named Hope. Bill's father died tragically in a car accident three months before his son was born. When Bill was four, his mother, Virginia, married a man named Roger Clinton. By the time Bill's half-brother, Roger, Jr., started school, Bill took his stepfather's name so he and Roger would both have the same last name.

The President's childhood was not always happy, but he strived to keep a positive outlook. Bill worked hard in school and was a top student. He also did volunteer work for local charities and played the saxophone in the school band. As a teenager he attended band camp every summer and once won a state saxophone competition.

THE ONCE AND FUTURE PRESIDENT

A friendly and outgoing student leader, 16-year-old Bill Clinton was chosen by the American Legion to attend Boy's Nation, a national youth conference in Washington, D.C. During the trip, he met President John F. Kennedy. It was a moment that Bill Clinton would treasure in years to come, and it was a turning point in his life. Bill had once thought about becoming a doctor or a musician. But after meeting President Kennedy he decided he wanted to serve in government. It was then that Bill Clinton first dreamed of someday becoming President of the United States.

After high school he attended Georgetown University. In 1968 he won a Rhodes scholarship and sailed off to England to study at Oxford University. When he returned home, he earned a law degree from Yale University. It was at Yale that he met Hillary Rodham, a top law student and an editor of the school's law review.

HILLARY'S STORY

Hillary Rodham Clinton was born in Chicago, Illinois, on October 27, 1947. She was the oldest of three children. She grew up in suburban Park Ridge where she was a top student, the president of her high school class, and an active Girl Scout. She attended Wellesley College, where she was elected president of the student government. After graduating, she decided to study law at Yale.

After law school Bill Clinton returned to Arkansas to teach law while Hillary went to Washington, where she worked for the Children's Defense Fund and as a staff member for a Congressional committee. She and Bill kept in close touch and visited each other often.

BILL AND HILLARY

In 1974, 28-year-old Bill Clinton ran for Congress in Arkansas. He campaigned hard, but lost.

A year later Hillary decided, as she later said, "to follow my heart to Arkansas." As the President tells it, he and Hillary were driving along one day when Hillary saw a house she said she liked. Not long after, Bill told Hillary, "I bought the house you liked. So you'd better marry me. I can't live there by myself."

Hillary and Bill Clinton were married in October 1975. Five years later, Bill and Hillary had a baby daughter whom they named Chelsea.

FROM THE STATE HOUSE
TO THE WHITE HOUSE

In 1978 Bill Clinton ran for governor of Arkansas and won, becoming the youngest governor in the nation's history. He eventually served five terms as governor. In a 1991 survey, Bill Clinton was named by his fellow governors as the country's most effective governor.

That same year Bill Clinton announced he would seek the presidency of the United States. He was a tireless campaigner. Bill, Hillary, and vice-presidential candidate Al Gore and his wife, Tipper, crisscrossed the country in a bus as candidate Clinton gave speech after speech until he was hoarse. In November 1992 voters made their choice. Bill Clinton became the country's 42nd President.

ALL ABOUT PRESIDENT CLINTON

The President's day is filled with meetings and appointments from dawn till dusk, but he still manages to pursue a variety of hobbies in his spare time. He likes to jog and is an avid reader. In addition to newspapers and countless government reports and documents, the President reads as many as four books a week. He also enjoys swimming, golf, and listening to music. The President has two saxophones, a tenor and an alto sax, but he doesn't get much time to play them!

A BUSY FIRST LADY

President Clinton has described his wife Hillary as a "First Lady of many talents." While living in Arkansas, Hillary served on a variety of committees that worked to improve health care and education. She now heads the Presidential Task Force on National Health Care Reform. In addition to overseeing arrangements for a variety of White House social events, the First Lady is also very involved in children's issues. Often, Hillary Clinton's schedule is as busy and event-filled as her husband's.

CHELSEA CLINTON: THE FIRST KID

In some ways, Chelsea Clinton has the hardest job of all. It's not easy being a kid in the White House! Everywhere Chelsea goes, she's trailed by reporters and Secret Service agents. However, Chelsea has managed to lead an almost typical teenager's life by becoming involved in all kinds of activities.

Chelsea loves dancing and attends regular ballet classes. She likes sports and plays soccer, softball (third base), and volleyball. Like most teenagers, she enjoys movies and visiting the mall. At home she enjoys playing card games and Ping-Pong with her parents.

Chelsea is a good student. She's thinking about becoming a scientist when she grows up. However, at the moment she has one major ambition — to have her friends sleep over at the White House!

SOCKS: AMERICA'S FIRST FELINE

When the Clintons lived in the governor's mansion in Little Rock, Arkansas, Chelsea asked her parents if she could get a pet. They said yes, and Chelsea chose a black and white cat she named Socks. Socks roamed free at the governor's mansion, but now he wanders around the White House lawn on a long leash. The First Family would like to let Socks run free, but they worry that he might somehow follow his instincts and try to return home to Little Rock! Lately, Socks has become a celebrity and is often trailed by photographers. Socks is definitely the country's top cat!

FAMILY MATTERS

The Clintons are a close family. The President, the First Lady, and Chelsea try to spend some part of every day together. Both President and Mrs. Clinton take time from their busy schedules to attend Chelsea's school events, dance recitals, and athletic events, where the President is known to cheer loudly for Chelsea's team!

There's a lot of togetherness in this First Family. "We're a little family," President Clinton is fond of saying, "but a powerful one." And when the President says that, he's not talking about political power!

Library of Congress Cataloging-in-Publication Data

Eliot, Chip.
    The Clintons: meet the First Family / Chip Eliot.
      p.   cm.
    ISBN 0-8167-3243-4 (lib. bdg.)
    1. Clinton, Bill, 1946-   —Juvenile literature. 2. Clinton, Hillary Rodham—
Juvenile literature. 3. Clinton family—Juvenile literature. 4. Presidents—United
States—Biography—Juvenile literature. 5. Presidents' wives—United States—
Biography—Juvenile literature. [1. Clinton, Bill, 1946-   2. Clinton, Hillary
Rodham. 3. Presidents. 4. First ladies.] I. Title.
E886.E45 1994
973.929 '092 '2——dc20
[B]   93-14027

Photo credits:

Photos on pages 3 and 9 © Allan Tannenbaum/Sygma;
page 5 © Art Meripol/Sygma; page 7 © Sygma;
page 11 © Jerry Staley/Sygma; pages 13, 15, 17, and
21 © AP/Wide World Photos; pages 19 and 23
© Ira Wyman/Sygma.

Cover photo © AP/Wide World Photos.